simply beautiful

GlorySound

A Division of Shawnee Press, Inc.
Exclusively Distributed by Hal Leonard Corporation

Visit Hal Leonard Online at **www.halleonard.com**
and Shawnee Press at **www.shawneepress.com**

Honoring Jenny Zachary for 10 years as a church pianist at Southeast Baptist Church, Murfreesboro, TN

What a Friend We Have in Jesus

Tune: **CONVERSE**
Music by CHARLES C. CONVERSE
Arranged by
MARY McDONALD (ASCAP)

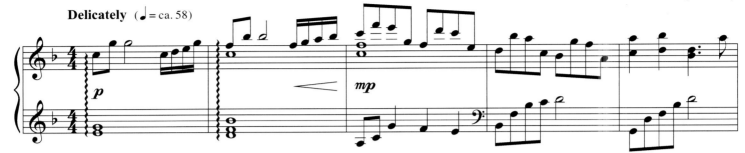

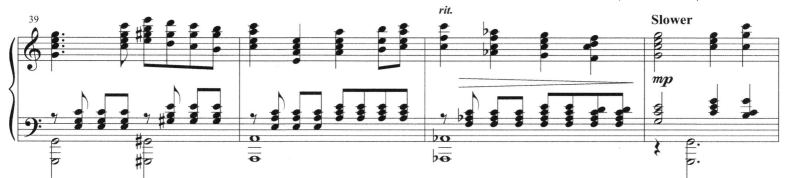

WHAT A FRIEND WE HAVE IN JESUS

Be Thou My Vision

Tune: **SLANE**
Music: Irish melody
Arranged by
CINDY BERRY (ASCAP)

Slowing to end

BE THOU MY VISION

for Jenna Stewart Baukovic

'Tis So Sweet to Trust in Jesus

with *Only Trust Him*

Tune: **TRUST IN JESUS**
Music by WILLIAM J. KIRKPATRICK
Arranged by
CAROLYN HAMLIN (ASCAP)

With much expression ($\quarternote$ = 88)

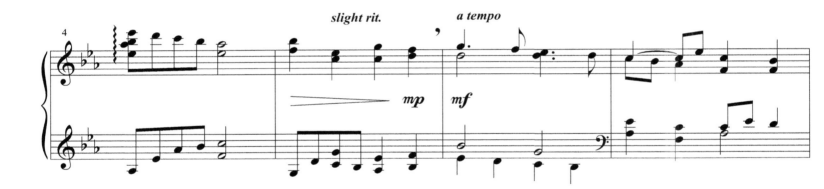

'TIS SO SWEET TO TRUST IN JESUS

'TIS SO SWEET TO TRUST IN JESUS

'TIS SO SWEET TO TRUST IN JESUS

I Am Bound for the Promised Land

Tune: **PROMISED LAND**
Music: Traditional American melody
Arranged by
LYNETTE MAYNARD (ASCAP)

I AM BOUND FOR THE PROMISED LAND

Resolute

slowing to the end

I AM BOUND FOR THE PROMISED LAND

Shades of Dawn

"...and I will give you the Morning Star!" Revelation 2:28

HARRY STRACK (ASCAP)

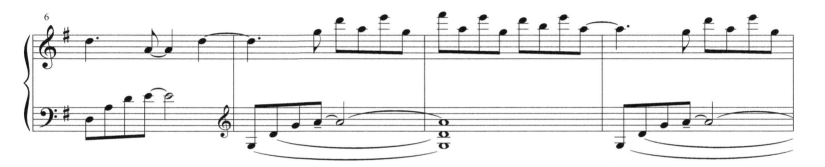

SHADES OF DAWN

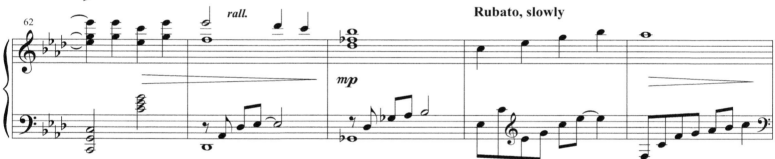

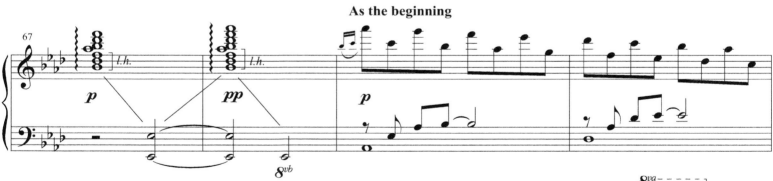

SHADES OF DAWN

Softly and Tenderly

Tune: **THOMPSON**
Music by WILL L. THOMPSON
Arranged by
SHIRLEY BRENDLINGER (ASCAP)

SOFTLY AND TENDERLY

SOFTLY AND TENDERLY

I Am His, and He Is Mine

Tune: **EVERLASTING LOVE**
Music by JAMES MOUNTAIN
Arranged by
DAN FORREST (ASCAP)

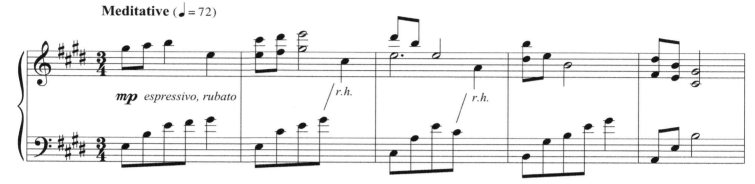

I AM HIS, AND HE IS MINE

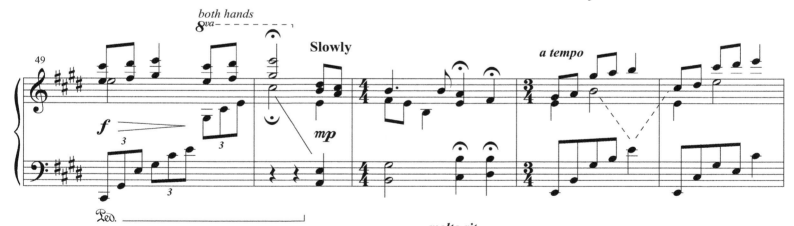

I AM HIS, AND HE IS MINE

Jesus, Keep Me Near the Cross

Tune: **NEAR THE CROSS**
Music by WILLIAM H. DOANE
Arranged by
VICKI TUCKER COURTNEY (ASCAP)

With a gentle lilt (♩ = ca. 104)

JESUS, KEEP ME NEAR THE CROSS

JESUS, KEEP ME NEAR THE CROSS

Shall We Gather at the River

Tune: **HANSON PLACE**
Music by ROBERT LOWRY
Arranged by
PATTI DRENNAN (ASCAP)

Flowing, with rubato (♩ = 72)

pedal harmonically

bring out melody

Copyright © 2010 HAL LEONARD CORPORATION
International Copyright Secured. All rights reserved.

SHALL WE GATHER AT THE RIVER

With movement

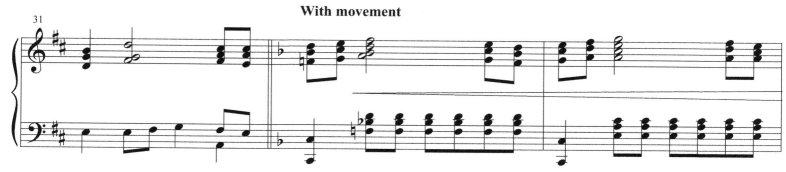

rit.   **With strength** (♩ = ca. 68)

ten.

rit.

SHALL WE GATHER AT THE RIVER

Beautiful

HEATHER SORENSON (ASCAP)

Molto espressivo

As the beginning

Slowly

BEAUTIFUL

dedicated to Joni V.

A Reflection on the Cross

Tune: **HAMBURG**
Music by LOWELL MASON
Arranged by
HEATHER SORENSON (ASCAP)

A REFLECTION ON THE CROSS

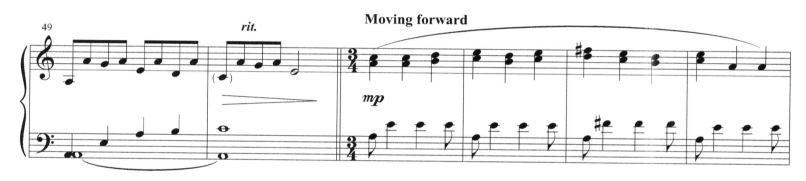

A REFLECTION ON THE CROSS

A REFLECTION ON THE CROSS

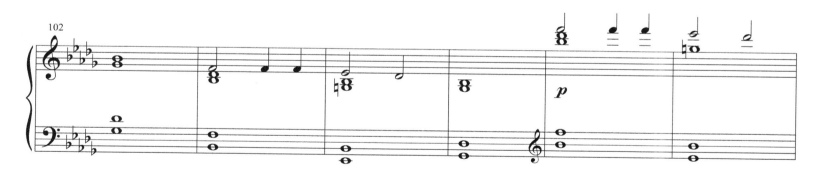

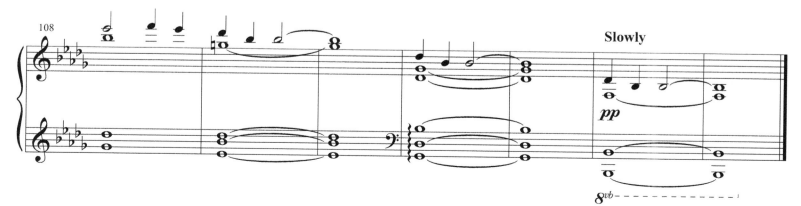

A REFLECTION ON THE CROSS

Learning to Walk

(Aubrey's Song)

JOSEPH M. MARTIN (BMI)

LEARNING TO WALK

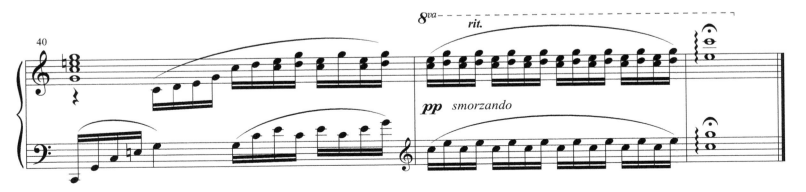

LEARNING TO WALK

The Solid Rock

Tune: **SOLID ROCK**
Music by WILLIAM B. BRADBURY
Arranged by
LLOYD LARSON (ASCAP)

A little slower

THE SOLID ROCK

We're Marching to Zion

Tune: **MARCHING TO ZION**
Music by ROBERT LOWRY
Arranged by
CINDY BERRY (ASCAP)

With confidence (♩. = 72)

WE'RE MARCHING TO ZION

I Surrender All

Tune: **SURRENDER**
Music by WINFIELD S. WEEDEN
Arranged by
STAN PETHEL (ASCAP)

With reflection; not too fast

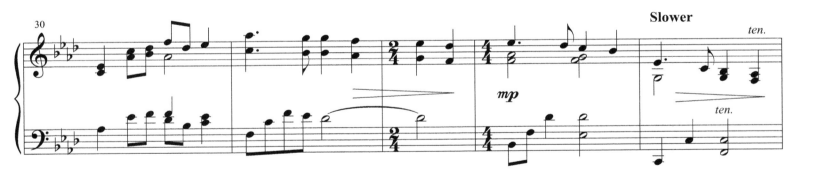

I SURRENDER ALL

Praise to the Lord, the Almighty

Tune: **LOBE DEN HERREN**
Music: Stralsund Gesangbuch, 1665
Arranged by
SHIRLEY BRENDLINGER (ASCAP)

Sensitively (♩ = 152)

senza ped.

gracefully

Warmly (♩ = 144)

con ped.

PRAISE TO THE LORD, THE ALMIGHTY

PRAISE TO THE LORD, THE ALMIGHTY

My Faith Looks Up to Thee

Tune: **OLIVET**
Music by LOWELL MASON
Arranged by
BRAD NIX (ASCAP)

Simply and sincerely (♩ = ca. 80)

MY FAITH LOOKS UP TO THEE

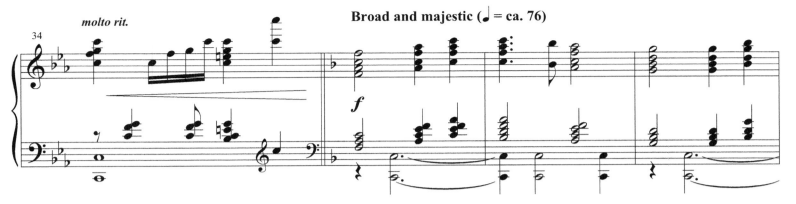

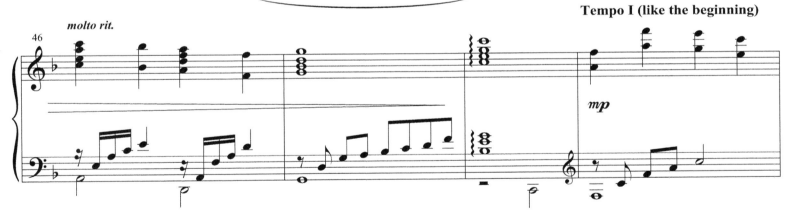

MY FAITH LOOKS UP TO THEE

There Is a Fountain

Tune: **CLEANSING FOUNTAIN**
Music: Traditional American melody
Arranged by
BRAD NIX (ASCAP)

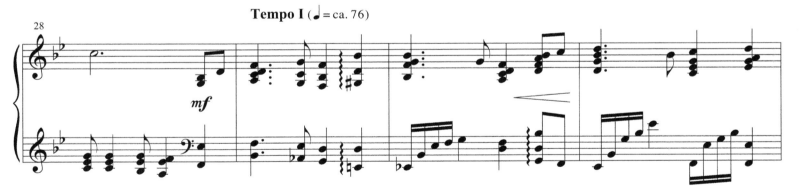

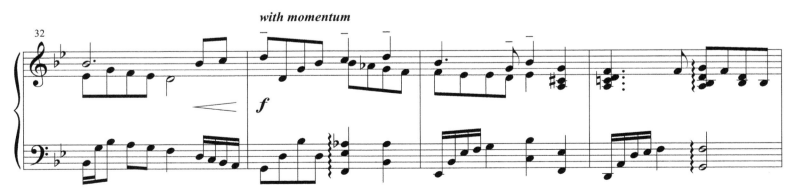

THERE IS A FOUNTAIN

THERE IS A FOUNTAIN

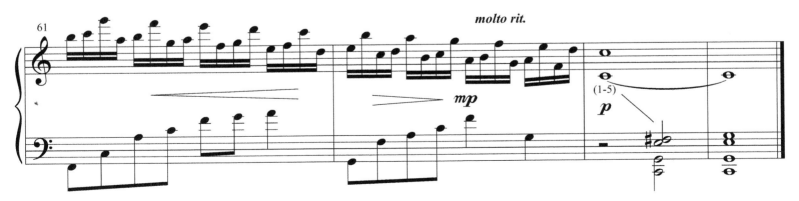

THERE IS A FOUNTAIN

to my son, Jonathan

Jonathan's Lullaby

JOSEPH M. MARTIN (BMI)

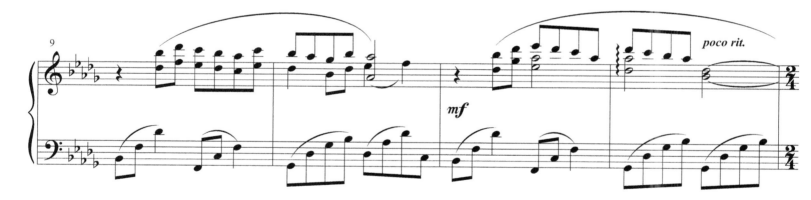

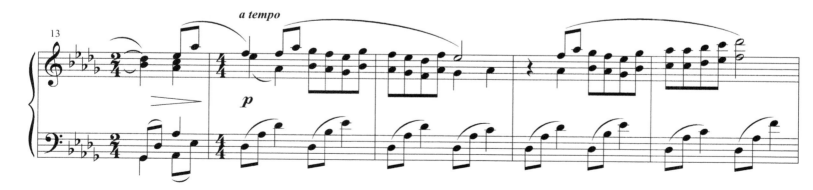

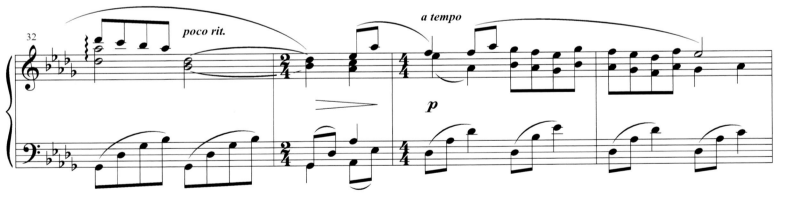

JONATHAN'S LULLABY

Contents

(Alphabetical Order)